Play Time!

Simon Tofield

CANONGATE

Edinburgh · London

To Amelia Shaw

Published by Canongate Books in 2013

1

Illustrations copyright © Simon Tofield, 2009-2013

The moral right of the author has been asserted

Simon's Cat (2009), Simon's Cat: Beyond the Fence (2010),
Simon's Cat in Kitten Chaos (2011) and Simon's Cat vs The World (2012)
were first published in Great Britain by Canongate Books Ltd.
14 High Street, Edinburgh EH1 1TE

www.canongate.tv

British Library Cataloguing-in-Publication Data
A catalogue record for this book is available on
request from the British Library

ISBN 978 0 85786 771 1

Printed and bound in Slovenia
by arrangement with Associated Agencies Oxford

For all your Simon's Cat goodies,
check out the webshop at

www.simonscat.com